The Urbana Free Library

To renew materials call
217-367-4057

5-08

DATE DUE		
AUG 14 2008	MAY 08 2009	
AUG 29 2008	NOV 09 2010	
SEP 20 2008	OCT 12 2011	
FEB 07 2009		
DEC 06 2010		
JAN 28 2011		

Beginner's Guide to
Drawn Thread
Embroidery

*To my daughter, Lauren Katie,
in the hope that her growing
love of embroidery will provide
her with as much pleasure in
her life as it has done in mine.*

Beginner's Guide to
Drawn Thread Embroidery

Patricia Bage

SEARCH PRESS

First published in Great Britain 2007

Search Press Limited
Wellwood, North Farm Road,
Tunbridge Wells, Kent TN2 3DR

Text and needlework designs copyright © Patricia Bage 2007

Photographs by Charlotte de la Bédoyère, Search Press Studios;
and Roddy Paine Photographic Studio.
Photographs and design copyright © Search Press Ltd 2007

ISBN-10: 1-84448-242-1
ISBN-13: 978-1-84448-242-9

The Publishers and author can accept no responsibility for any
consequences arising from the information, advice or instructions
given in this publication.

Readers are permitted to reproduce any of the designs in this book
for their personal use, or for the purposes of selling for charity,
free of charge and without the prior permission of the Publishers.
Any use of the designs for commercial purposes is not permitted
without the prior permission of the Publishers.

Suppliers

If you have difficulty in obtaining any of the materials and
equipment mentioned in this book, then please visit the Search
Press website for details of suppliers: www.searchpress.com

Alternatively, you can visit the author's website:
www.patricia-ann-designs.com
for a current list of stockists, including firms who operate a mail-
order service.

Publisher's note
All the step-by-step photographs in this book feature
the author, Patricia Bage, demonstrating drawn thread
embroidery. No models have been used.

Acknowledgements

*First and foremost, I would like to thank my husband
Brian, my sons David and Gary, and my daughter
Lauren for their love and support during the writing
and preparation of this book.*

*I would also like to thank Zweigart in the USA for
providing the linen fabric I have used to create the
embroideries in this book; Kreinik, USA for the silk
and metallic threads; DMC, UK for the stranded and
Perle cotton; Wichelt Imports, Inc., USA for providing
the Mill Hill beads and treasures; and Macleod Craft
Marketing, UK for supplying the Caron Waterlilies silk
threads. Thank you also to the manufacturers of the
computer program EasyGrapher Stitch Wiz, which I
used to create the stitch diagrams, and PremiumPlus
2000 with which I drew the patterns for the projects.*

*I am indebted to Linda Nelson, Melissa Campbell,
Deborah Somerlot, Kris Herber and Ellen Brittain in
the USA; Jennifer Lloyd in the UK; Debra Morris in
Canada; and Gail Phillips and Marianne Wohlk in
Australia for proofreading the projects. Thanks also to
Jenny Robinson, who completed the finishing of the bell
pull (page 41) and the cushion (pages 56–57), and
who provided the instructions for each.*

Front cover
Detail from Rosebud Trellis design (see page 59).

Page 1
Detail from decorative cushion, made using the Flower Garland
design (see pages 56–57).

Page 3
Detail from Summer Garden design (see page 41).

Page 5
Traditional whitework version of the Summer Garden design
(see page 45).

Contents

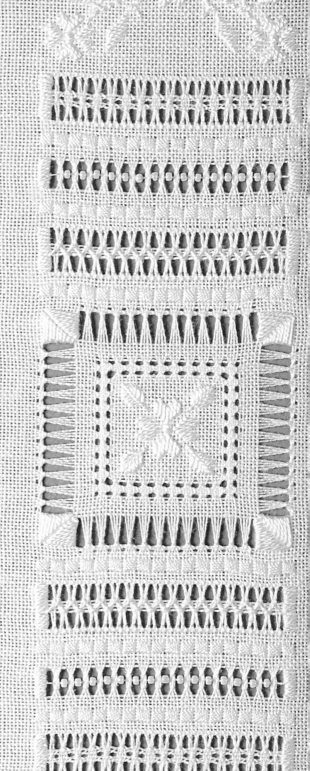

Introduction

Drawn thread work essentially involves cutting and withdrawing the fabric threads, leaving open areas in the ground fabric, which can then be embellished to create an intricate, lacy effect. Who would not be nervous the first time they cut the threads of their fabric? Even the most experienced stitcher has some trepidation before cutting their precious embroidery. This book will guide you through all the stages of drawn thread work, giving you the skills and confidence that will enable you to produce delicate and detailed embroideries of your own. These can then be framed, or made into decorative items such as box lids, cushions and bell pulls, each of which are described in this book.

Drawn thread is a counted thread technique, and one of the oldest forms of openwork embroidery. It was traditionally worked on linen. Through the centuries, many varieties of drawn thread work have evolved. In thirteenth-century Germany, drawn thread embroideries were stitched by nuns in convents to decorate altar cloths. During the Renaissance, drawn thread work became popular as a means of simulating true lace, which was expensive and painstakingly slow to produce. Garments were hemmed with ornamental hemstitching, and drawn thread work was used to trim wristbands and necklines, as well as being used to embellish household linens.

Many people confuse drawn thread work with pulled thread work, where the fabric threads are not cut but pulled to create a lacy effect. Both techniques are forms of openwork embroidery, and both can also be categorised under the term 'whitework'.

For the projects in this book, I have taken my inspiration from traditional band samplers of the seventeenth century. These featured counted thread embroidery stitches, and some also included areas of drawn thread work. By combining traditional stitches and techniques from the past with contemporary fibres, threads and embellishments, I hope to put a modern twist on this beautiful and historical form of embroidery that will inspire you to try it out for yourself.

Although I have recommended specific threads to be used in the projects, you can substitute these for which ever makes or colours you choose, but please be aware that the finished embroidery may differ from that shown.

Materials

The secret to drawn thread work is a good quality, evenweave fabric and a pair of sharp scissors. I also choose to embellish my work with high quality threads, beads and treasures. All the materials needed for the projects in this book can be purchased from any good needlework shop or via the internet.

Needles

I use tapestry needles for drawn thread embroidery. They have a blunt point that will not pierce the fabric, and a large eye. They are available in a variety of sizes, from No. 13 (the largest) to No. 28 (the smallest). For the projects in this book I suggest using a No. 26 when stitching with floss, silk fibres and Perle cotton 12, and a No. 24 when using Perle cotton 8 and metallic threads.

Beading needles are useful for sewing on beads, though a No. 26 or No. 28 tapestry needle would probably be small enough unless you are using petite beads. Beading needles are very thin, and either long or short. They have a very sharp point and a very small eye so that beads can slide down them easily.

Scissors

For drawn thread work, a good pair of embroidery scissors is essential. They need to be of good quality – sharp, with pointed blades and a good cutting edge that runs the full length of the blade.

It is worth considering having a separate pair of scissors for cutting metallic threads. They are very hard on scissors and will eventually blunt the cutting edges.

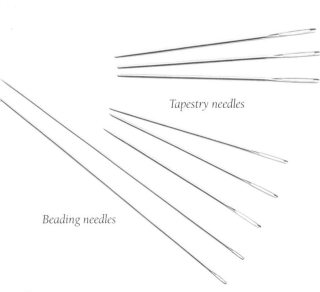

Tapestry needles

Beading needles

Frames and stands

I prefer to stitch with my fabric in a frame to ensure I have an even tension, though I do know people who can stitch without a frame. It is therefore a personal choice, and depends on which method you are most comfortable with. My favourite frame consists of four modular plastic tubes. The tubes come in a variety of lengths that you can fit together in which ever combination suits the shape and size of your embroidery. The fabric is stretched over the plastic tubes and held in place by a plastic clamp on each side. This does not mark the fabric, and keeps it really taut. You can loosen the fabric prior to cutting the fabric threads without having to remove it from the frame; just turn the clamps in towards the centre until the fabric is slack enough to allow you to comfortably cut the fabric threads. Once you have cut the fabric threads you can tighten the fabric again by turning the clamps back in the opposite direction. Unlike traditional wooden quilters' frames, you do not need to sew the fabric on to the frame.

Other popular frames are stretcher bars, hoops and scroll frames. Attaching your frame to either a table stand or a floor stand will enable you to have both hands free to work. Again, this is a personal preference. Many stands also include a light and a magnifying glass.

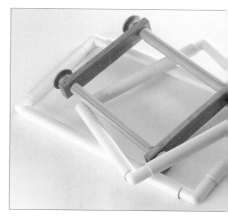

A selection of frames suitable for drawn thread work.

Fabric

All the projects in this book are stitched on evenweave linen. The term 'evenweave' means that the fabric has the same number of vertical (warp) threads as horizontal (weft) threads. Throughout the centuries, linen has been a popular choice for all types of needlework, including counted thread work and samplers. As linen is a natural fibre, the threads can vary slightly in thickness, and sometimes you will find slubs in the fabric. This adds to its authentic look. Modern speciality evenweave fabrics can be a mixture of linen and cotton. These are cheaper than pure linen and the weave of the fabric threads is uniform and without slubs.

In this book I have used linen fabrics that are either 28ct (28 threads per inch of the fabric) or 25ct (25 threads per inch), though you could use a speciality evenweave if you prefer. Aida is not a suitable fabric for the projects in this book.

Threads

Floss is a six-stranded cotton embroidery thread, and is the most common thread used for all types of embroidery. It has a natural sheen and is available in hundreds of colours. I generally use two strands of thread for cross stitch and speciality stitches, and one strand of thread for backstitching. **Silk thread** is also a stranded thread with a natural sheen. It is stronger and smoother than standard floss and is beautiful to work with, though it is more expensive.

Overdyed threads are also a stranded thread, either silk or cotton, that has been dyed several colours to produce a variegated effect. The colours may be from the same colour family, progressing from light to dark, or may include different colours blended together. Many of these threads are dyed by hand. When stitching with overdyed threads, use two strands of thread as they come off the skein, and complete each stitch before moving on to the next one to obtain the full effect of the colour changes. Do not use the loop method (see page 17) to begin stitching.

Perle cotton is a strong thread, ideal for drawn thread work. It is a two-ply, non-separable, twisted thread that has a lustrous sheen. The largest size is 3, decreasing in order to 5, 8 and, the smallest, 12. Here size refers to the thickness of the thread. In the projects in this book, I have used Perle 5, 8 and 12.

I use **metallic braid** to give a sparkly finish to my work. It is used as it comes off the spool, and you do not separate the strands. It is a round thread that has a bright metallic sheen. In this book I have used Very Fine Braid No. 4 and Fine Braid No. 8; it is also available in Nos 12, 16 and 32. It comes in many colours, including fluorescent and luminescent colours. Other metallic threads include blending filaments, Japan threads, cords, cable and ribbon.

Beads, crystal and glass treasures

Beads come in a variety of sizes and colours and add extra detail and sparkle to a design. I have used **seed beads** and **petite beads** in the projects in this book. I have also used **crystal** and **glass treasures**.

Other equipment

There are a number of other needlework accessories you may find useful, but which are not essential. These include a **tape measure**; a pair of **round-ended scissors** for cutting metallic threads; a **'parking lot magnet'**, which is a pair of magnets that you place either side of your fabric to provide a safe place for your needles when you are not stitching; a **'boo boo stick'**, which is a small, double-ended brush that helps you remove stitches without damaging the fabric; a pair of speciality **needlework tweezers**, which will help you remove both cut fabric threads and stitching errors; a **'bead nabber'**, used to help pick up beads; **laying tools** to keep satin stitches neat and parallel; a **needle threader**; a **magnifying glass** for detailed work; **thread conditioner**, to smooth your thread and help prevent tangling and fraying; a **thread winder**, used to keep your threads neat and tidy; a **'dololly'**, which is a useful tool for tidying up very small threads on the reverse of your stitching when they are too short for a regular needle; **counting pins**, to help you count the fabric threads accurately, which is an essential part of drawn thread work; and a **pin cushion**.

To keep all of your threads neat and tidy I suggest using a **floss storage box**, which is a lidded box divided into small sections that are large enough to hold reels and skeins of thread. Finally, drawn thread work is so precise that good light is essential. You may wish to invest in a purpose-made **stitching light** that works with a natural daylight bulb; many of these lamps are also fitted with a magnifying glass.

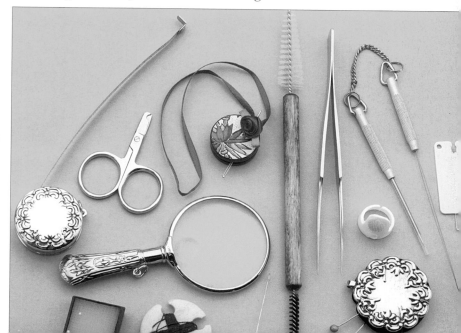

Before you stitch

The first thing you will need to do when starting an embroidery is to cut out the fabric. This needs to be 8cm (3in) wider on each side than the finished piece. For example, if the finished size is 8 x 26cm (3 x 10in) the fabric should be cut to 24 x 42cm (9 x 16in).

Natural linen is very prone to creasing, so I like to iron the fabric before I start stitching. To make ironing easier, I first wash the linen in warm water using a very small amount of hand-wash detergent (not washing-up liquid), and afterwards rinse it thoroughly with cold water. Wrap the fabric in a clean, white, fluffy towel and gently squeeze out as much moisture as possible without twisting or wringing the fabric. Finally, place another clean, dry towel on an ironing board, lay the linen on the towel (wrong-side down if you have already started stitching), place a piece of muslin over the top and iron until the linen is dry.

Linen fabrics will fray, but do not hem the edges; if you accidentally cut the wrong thread, you will need to be able to take a thread from the edge of the fabric to repair your mistake. You are now ready to start stitching.

The secret to drawn thread work on linen is careful counting, so it is advisable to mark the outline of the area to be stitched with basting stitches. These stitches will make your counting easier, and are removed once the sampler is completed.

> ### Tip
> If you need to wash your fabric again after you have started stitching, follow the same method, but check that any overdyed threads you have used are washable.

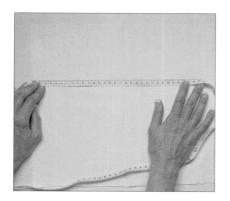

> ### Tip
> Basting stitches are evenly worked running stitches, going over and under two threads at a time (see page 31).

1. First, find the central vertical thread of your piece of fabric, either by folding it in half and marking the centre with a pin, or by measuring with a tape measure (as shown above).

2. Using one strand of a light-coloured floss, place two or three basting stitches to mark the centre line, approximately 4cm (1½in) from one edge of the fabric. Leave the working thread on the needle.

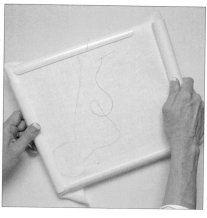

3. Secure the fabric in a frame, making sure it is taut and evenly stretched across the frame.

4. Continue basting to the opposite edge of the frame.

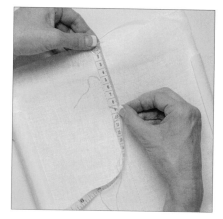

5. Unclip the top of the frame, and measure 8cm (3in) down the central line from the edge of the fabric. Mark the point with a needle. This is the centre point of the top line of your embroidery.

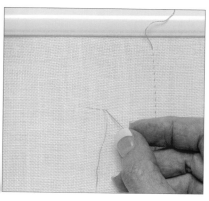

6. Replace the frame, and carefully count the threads to the left of the centre point, so if the design is eighty threads wide, count forty threads to the left. Mark this point, and baste back to the centre line.

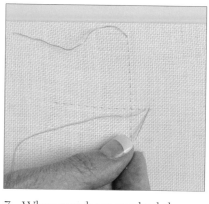

7. When you have reached the centre, count forty threads to the right and continue basting.

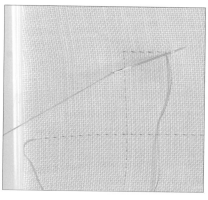

8. When you have completed the top horizontal line, turn your fabric through 90° and baste the right-hand vertical line, counting the threads as you go.

9. Complete the outline. Leave the centre line in for now, removing it later as you work.

Cutting the fabric threads

The first and most important tip that I can offer is to always cut in a good light and when you are not tired! Everyone feels nervous about cutting their fabric threads, especially if you have already completed a large section of stitching.

This book shows two different methods of preparing the fabric before cutting. The first technique involves cutting and reweaving the fabric threads to secure them, and the second uses satin stitch blocks as security stitches. Both of these methods are described below.

Cutting and reweaving the fabric threads

When cutting and reweaving the fabric threads, I only cut two fabric threads at a time. This helps with counting and prevents me accidentally cutting a wrong thread. If you cut too many threads at one time you are more likely to make an error. If you are stitching on a frame, always loosen or remove the fabric before you begin cutting, and always work with the right side of the fabric facing up.

1. Place the scissors under two fabric threads in the centre of the design and cut.

2. Using the tip of a needle, carefully unweave one of the cut fabric threads. Work towards the left-hand margin.

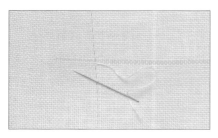

4. Stop unweaving the second cut fabric thread at the margin and thread it through a needle.

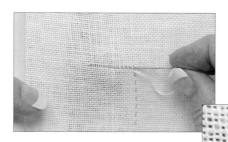

5. Reweave the thread through the gap left by the first thread to the left of the basting stitches, taking care to follow the weave of the fabric.

3. Unweave the thread to approximately 2.5cm (1in) past the margin, and pass the end of the thread through to the back of the fabric. Carefully start to unweave the second thread. You will be using this thread for reweaving, so it is important that it does not break.

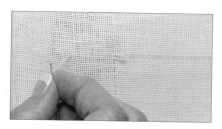

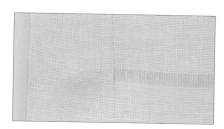

6. Pull the thread through, not too tightly otherwise it could break or the fabric could become puckered.

7. Pass the thread through to the back of the fabric for a tidy finish.

8. Continue cutting and reweaving two threads at a time for as many rows as the pattern demands, then turn your work through 180° and repeat for the right-hand side.

Satin stitch blocks

When using satin stitch blocks for securing cut threads, it is an easy mistake to misalign the satin stitch blocks, or to incorrectly count the number of satin stitches in a block. Before you begin cutting, therefore, make sure that each fabric thread that is going to be cut has a satin stitch at either end, and that there is one extra satin stitch beyond the top and bottom of the fabric threads that are to be cut. I would suggest that you cut and remove one pair of threads at a time. You are then less likely to make an error.

1. Make a satin stitch block at each end of the threads to be cut. Check that they are in line by running a needle along the fabric from one end to the other, without crossing a horizontal thread.

2. Loosen the fabric in the frame a little, and place the lower blade of your scissors into the same hole as the last satin stitch in the right-hand block. Make sure there are two fabric threads on the blade, and manoeuvre the scissors as close as possible to the stitches.

3. Angle the cutting edge towards the satin stitches, and cut. Repeat for all the threads in the block, cutting two threads at a time.

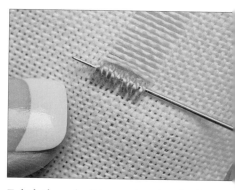

4. Rotate the fabric and cut the other ends of the fabric threads in the same way. Start to remove the cut threads using the tip of a tapestry needle, taking care not to damage the fabric.

5. Continue removing all the cut threads between the two satin stitch blocks.

To hide the ends of the cut threads, take the fabric out of the frame, slide a needle under the satin stitch block and gently push the stitches towards the gap.

15

Threading a needle with Perle cotton

1. Wrap the thread around your forefinger and press firmly on it with the eye of a needle.

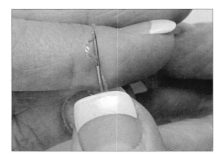

2. Rub the needle firmly up and down, drawing the thread up into a loop.

3. Pull the thread through the eye.

Threading a needle with metallic thread

1. Make a loop in the thread.

2. Push the loop through the eye of the needle.

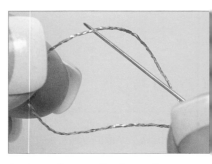

3. Pass the needle through the loop.

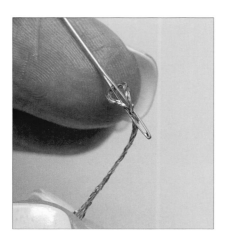

4. Pull the thread tight to form a knot. This secures the needle on the thread and prevents the thread from slipping through the eye.

Beginning a stitch

I use a waste knot to hold the thread in place while I am sewing, cutting and removing it once the stitching is complete. Make a small knot in the end of the thread, and place a single small stitch approximately 8cm (3in) from the start of your stitching. Bring the needle through to the front of the fabric to begin sewing.

To secure a working thread at the side of a block of drawn threads, make sure the waste knot is placed level with the point at which you wish to start stitching, and about 8cm (3in) from it. As you take the working thread across the back of your work, keep it parallel with the horizontal fabric threads. Attach it carefully to a few vertical threads, at points where they cross the horizontal thread. Make sure the working thread remains invisible on the right side of the fabric. Remember that where there is a satin stitch block either side of the drawn thread area, the satin stitch blocks can be used to secure the working thread.

Another way of beginning a stitch is to use the loop method. Take a single thread, fold it in half, and thread the two ends through a needle. Make a stitch in the fabric, passing the needle through the loop on the back. This method should not be used with overdyed threads.

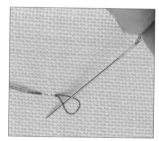

Beginning a stitch with a waste knot.

Beginning a stitch with a loop.

Ending a stitch

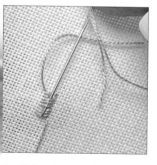

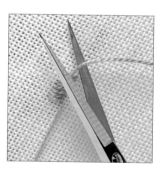

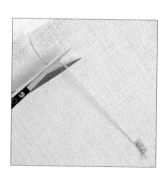

1. Take the working thread through to the back of the fabric, and pass it underneath three or four stitches.

2. Pull the thread through and pass it back under the stitches in the opposite direction.

3. Cut off the end of the thread.

4. Cut off and remove the waste knot.

5. Weave the tail thread through the back of the embroidery and trim it off.

Drawn thread techniques

In drawn thread work, the fabric threads are cut and withdrawn, leaving open areas in the fabric. If only the horizontal (weft) threads are cut and withdrawn, this leaves the vertical (warp) threads loose. In this section, I describe various techniques for drawing the loose fabric threads into groups to produce a decorative border. When working a square design (such as the one on pages 52–53), both horizontal and vertical threads are cut and withdrawn. Always start at the bottom right-hand corner of the drawn threads and work left, unless stated otherwise.

Hemstitch over two threads

Hemstitch has been used for centuries as a decorative hem for needlework items such as table linens, bed linens and clothing, and is featured in samplers. This simple form of hemstitch is used to gather threads into groups of two.

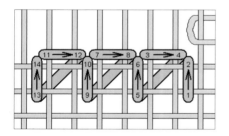

Hemstitch over two threads.

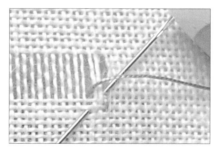

1. Come up through the fabric at 1 and go down at 2. Take the needle behind the first two vertical fabric threads and bring it up at 3, then take it back down at 4 (through the same space as 2). Bring the needle up at 5.

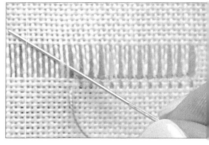

2. Pull the thread firmly to create a small backstitch that draws the two vertical fabric threads together. Continue in the same way along the row.

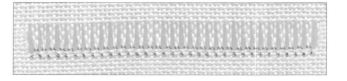

The completed stitch.

Hemstitch over four threads

This is worked in the same way as the previous stitch, but this time the fabric threads are gathered together in groups of four.

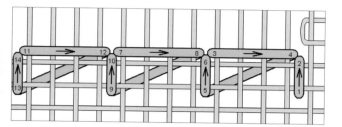

Hemstitch over four threads.

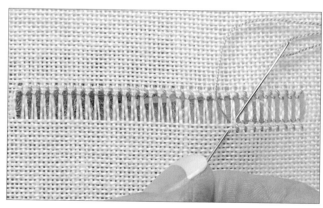

The completed stitch.

Ladder stitch

This stitch comprises two rows of hemstitch worked along the upper and lower edges of a block of drawn threads. The two rows correspond exactly so that the threads are gathered into vertical bars that resemble a ladder, which gives the stitch its name. It can be used as a decorative border, and is also the foundation stitch for a number of other stitches featured in this book.

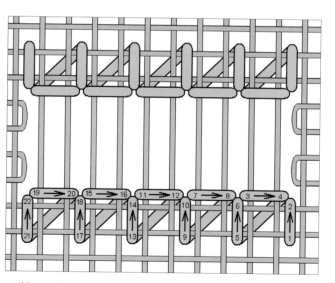

Ladder stitch.

1. Work hemstitch over two vertical threads along one edge of the drawn threads, then turn the fabric through 180° and work the second row.

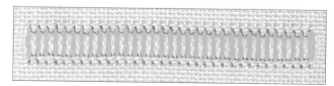

The completed ladder stitch.

Zig zag hemstitch

This stitch is also known as serpentine hemstitch or trellis hemstitch. In zig zag hemstitch, the groups of threads in the upper and lower rows do not correspond.

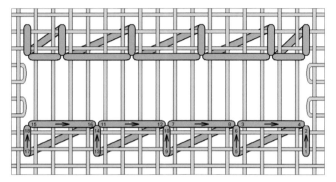

Zig zag hemstitch.

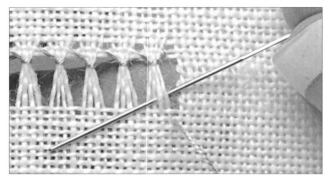

1. Work one row in hemstitch over four threads (see page 19). Turn the fabric through 180° and start the second row by working the first stitch over two threads.

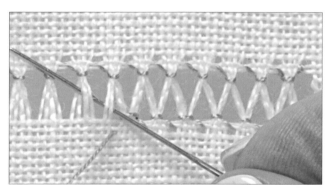

2. Work the remaining stitches in hemstitch over four threads. By gathering two vertical threads from one group and two from the next, you will produce a zig zag pattern. You will complete the row with a group of two vertical threads.

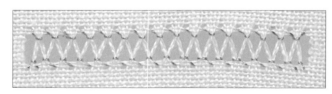

The completed stitch.

Interlaced hemstitch

This is a decorative variation of ladder stitch. Begin by following the instructions for ladder stitch on page 19.

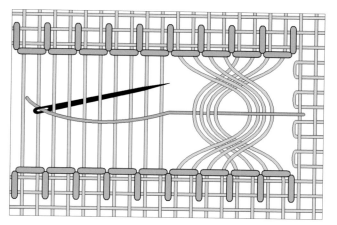

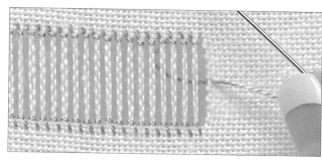

Interlaced hemstitch.

1. Work ladder stitch along the upper and lower edges of the block of drawn threads. Beginning at the right-hand side, anchor the working thread in the centre of the margin.

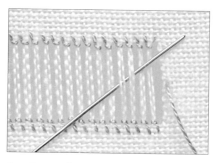

2. Count four groups of fabric threads (eight threads in total), and take the needle down after the eighth thread, then back up between the fourth and the fifth.

3. Twist the point of the needle round to the left and take it back down to the right of the first vertical thread. The group of threads will flip over each other.

4. Continue twisting the needle to the left and bring it back up just before the ninth vertical thread.

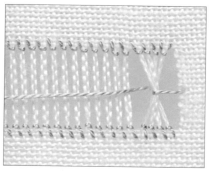

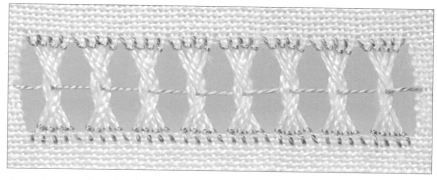

5. Pull the working thread firmly so the threads stay in position.

A complete row of interlaced hemstitch. At the end of the row, secure the thread at the left-hand margin.

Interlaced hemstitch with beads

This is a variation of interlaced hemstitch. First, the ladder stitch along the upper and lower edges is omitted, so the threads are not drawn into groups before interlacing, and secondly, a bead is placed between each group of interlaced threads.

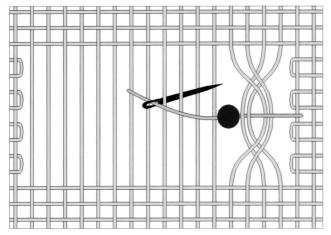

Interlaced hemstitch with beads.

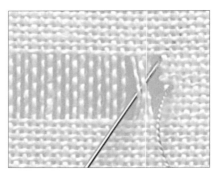

1. Anchor the working thread in the centre of the right-hand margin. Count four vertical threads along, and take the needle down after the fourth thread, then back up between the second and third.

2. Twist the needle to the left as you did on page 21 steps 3 and 4, pull the working thread firmly to hold the vertical threads in place, and add a bead.

3. Push the bead down so it lies after the first stitch, and form the second stitch in the same way.

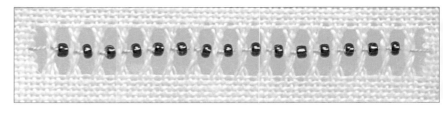

A complete row of interlaced hemstitch with beads. At the end of the row, secure the thread at the left-hand margin.

Diamond hemstitch

This stitch is worked over four horizontal fabric threads, between two bands of drawn threads. Begin by working hemstitch over two threads along the upper edge of the top band, and the lower edge of the bottom band.

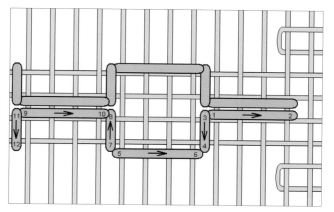

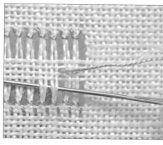

Diamond hemstitch.

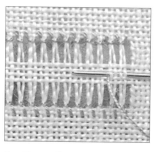

1. Begin by counting four threads in from the right-hand margin, bring the needle up at 1, down at 2, then back up at 3 (through the same hole as 1).

2. Pull the thread tight, and pass the needle down at 4 and back up at 5, behind four vertical threads.

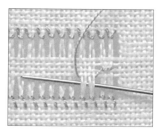

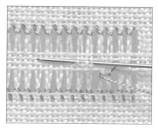

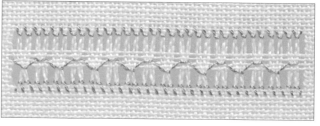

3. Take the working thread over the four vertical threads, pass the needle back through the fabric at 6 (the same space as 4), and back up at 7 (the same space as 5).

4. Draw the four vertical threads into a bundle and begin the next stitch by taking the needle down at 8 and up four threads along at 9.

5. Complete the first row of diamond hemstitch.

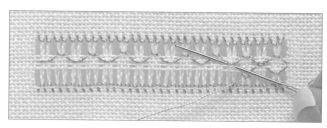

6. Turn the fabric through 180° and start the second row. Work the stitches as a mirror image of those in the first row; work the vertical stitches into the same holes as those of the first row.

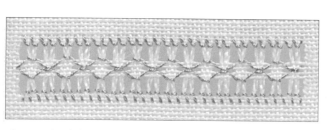

The completed diamond hemstitch.

Herringbone stitch

Herringbone stitch is also known as Russian cross or plaited stitch. It is a common feature of samplers and has many variations. In this book, I have used the stitch over four horizontal fabric threads between two bands of drawn threads. When working this stitch, the reverse of the fabric resembles two rows of running stitch. These stitches pull the vertical fabric threads into groups to form the pattern. Unlike the previous stitches in this section, this one is worked left to right. Begin by working hemstitch over two threads along the upper edge of the top band, and the lower edge of the bottom band of drawn threads.

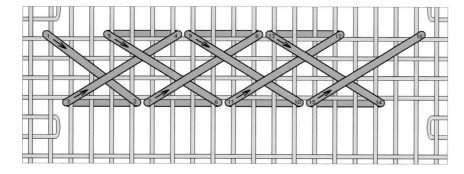

Herringbone stitch.

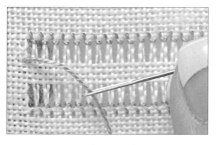

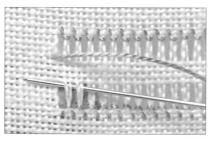

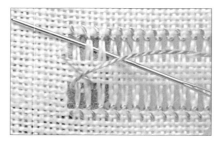

1. Starting in the top left-hand corner, bring the needle up just to the left of the first uncut vertical thread, and just below the first reweaved horizontal thread.

2. Take the thread diagonally across the vertical fabric threads, then pass the needle down at 2, take it behind four fabric threads and bring it up at 3.

3. Gather the four threads into a bundle. Take the thread diagonally across six vertical threads, and pass the needle down at 4 and bring it up at 5.

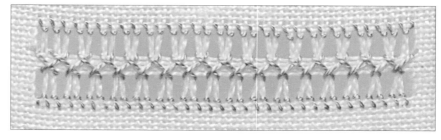

4. Gather the four threads together, and continue working in the same pattern along the row.

The completed herringbone stitch.

Coral knots

Coral knots are used to gather groups of loose fabric threads into secondary groups, known as clusters. In this demonstration, I have begun by using a four-sided stitch (see page 36) to gather the vertical threads into groups of four. Alternatively, use ladder stitch over four threads. The first coral knot is worked over two threads and the remainder over four, two from each adjacent group, creating a diamond pattern.

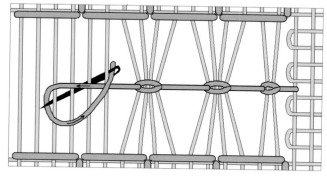

Coral knots.

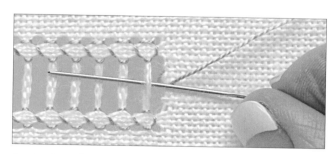

1. Anchor the working thread in the centre of the right-hand margin. Pass the needle behind the first two vertical threads.

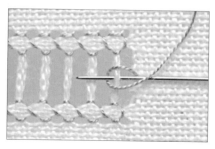

2. Loop the working thread around the needle.

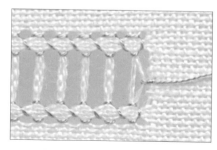

3. Pull the thread into a knot.

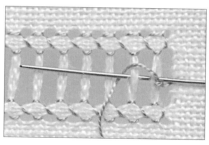

4. Work the next knot over four threads, two from the first group and two from the next.

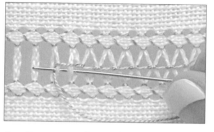

5. Continue along the row, keeping the working thread taut and gathering the threads into clusters of four. End with two threads.

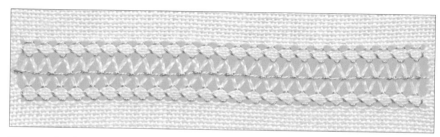

The completed row of coral knots.

Modified coral knot clusters

In this version of coral knots, ladder stitch is first worked over two threads, then coral knots used to gather the threads into clusters. Further coral knots are then used to create a more detailed pattern.

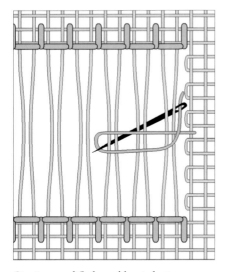

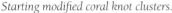

Starting modified coral knot clusters.

1. Anchor the working thread in the centre of the right-hand margin, pass the needle behind six vertical threads (three groups of threads) and loop the working thread under the tip of the needle.

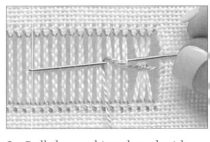

2. Pull the working thread with a medium tension, and work the next coral knot in the same way.

3. Continue gathering the groups of threads into clusters of three as you work along the row. Secure the thread to finish. This row is referred to as the horizontal thread.

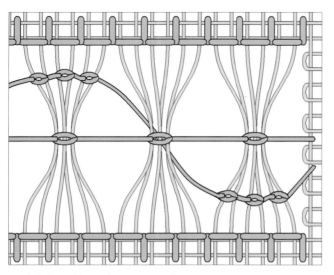

Modified coral knot clusters, second stage.

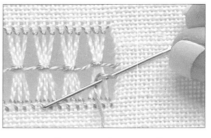

4. Start the second stage of modified coral knot stitch using a new thread. Secure it two holes below the centre of the right-hand margin. Form a coral knot over the first two vertical threads, about halfway down.

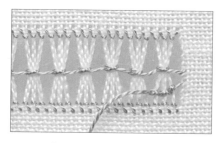

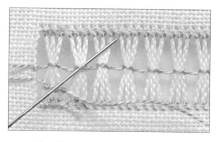

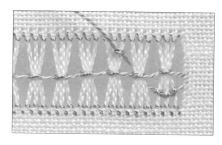

5. Work two further coral knots over the remaining two pairs of threads in the first cluster.

6. Take the thread through to the back of the fabric and pass the needle up through the back of the second coral knot in the horizontal thread.

7. Bring the needle back through to the front of your work and form a coral knot over the first pair of threads in the third cluster.

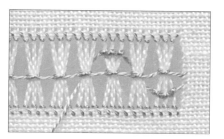

8. Make coral knots over the remaining two pairs of threads in the cluster, and pass the thread through the back of the fourth coral knot in the horizontal thread.

9. Continue working in the same pattern to the end of the row. Secure the thread to finish.

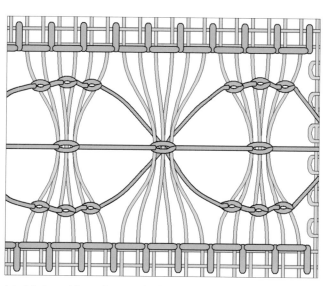

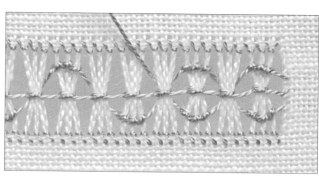

10. Start the third stage of modified coral knot stitch using a new thread. Secure it two holes above the centre of the right-hand margin and work the row as a mirror image of the previous one.

Modified coral knot clusters, third stage.

The completed modified coral knot clusters.

Woven wheels

To work this stitch, both the horizontal and vertical threads are cut and reweaved to create an open space. In this demonstration, I have started with interlaced hemstitch worked across the vertical and horizontal blocks of drawn threads.

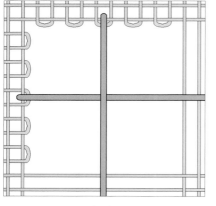

Starting a woven wheel.

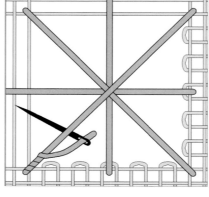

Overcasting the diagonals.

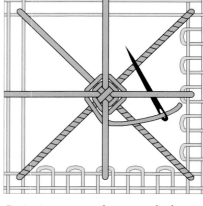

Beginning to weave the woven wheel.

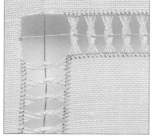

1. Work interlaced hemstitch across the horizontal and vertical blocks of drawn threads, in each case taking the working thread across the open space and securing it on the other side.

2. Turn the fabric so that the open space is positioned top right, and work a cross stitch so that a double cross is formed over it.

3. Turn the fabric so that the open space is positioned bottom right, and overcast the last diagonal you made by wrapping the working thread around it. Maintain tension on the wrapping thread using your other hand.

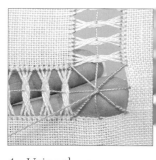

4. Using the same working thread, overcast the other diagonal leg to the centre only.

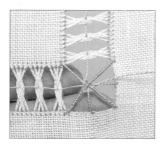

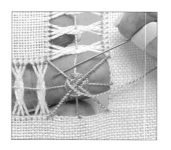

5. Start weaving the thread over and under the 'spokes' of the wheel. Work from the centre of the wheel outwards in an anticlockwise direction to form a circular pattern.

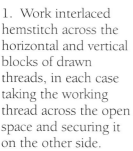

6. When the woven wheel is the desired size, finish by overcasting the second half of the diagonal stitch. Take the thread to the back of the fabric when you have finished, and secure it.

Beadwork

Beads and treasures can add extra texture, detail and sparkle to a design. I prefer to leave beadwork until last, once all the other stitching is completed. (This does not apply to interlaced hemstitch with beads, in which the beads are threaded on as you work the stitch.)

Attach beads with a single strand of floss that matches the colour of the fabric, though if you are using transparent beads, their colour may change depending on the colour of the thread used.

Beading needles have a very sharp point and a small eye, which can make them difficult to thread. A No. 26 tapestry needle is small enough for sewing on seed beads, but if you are using petite beads you will have to use a beading needle.

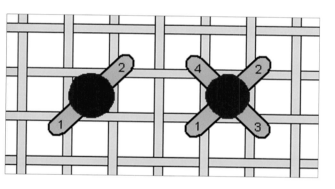

Beads attached using a half cross stitch and a full cross stitch (see page 32).

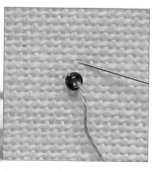

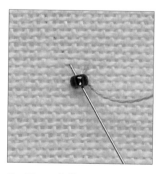

1. Bring the needle up through the fabric (1), pick up a bead and push it to the end of the thread, then take the needle back down on the diagonal, at 2.

2. Tighten the thread.

3. For a full cross stitch, work a second stitch across the other diagonal (3–4).

4. Pull the thread tight.

Embroidery stitches

Embroidery can be used to enhance any piece of drawn thread work by allowing you to add colour and texture to your design. For the projects in this book I have included a selection of basic counted thread embroidery stitches. Many of these stitches feature in needlepoint, and as they have evolved over the years in different countries, they have been given different names. The ones I have demonstrated here are only a small selection of all those in existence, but with these you can produce endless varieties of patterns and designs in all different colours and using various types of thread. No embroidery stitches other than those shown here are used in the projects on pages 40–63.

Backstitch

Backstitching is also known as point de sable. It is used to add detail, or to outline a design. Backstitches are short, even stitches that can be worked horizontally, vertically or diagonally. Rows are worked left to right, though individual stitches are worked right to left over two fabric threads. In the following demonstration I have used a single strand of six-stranded cotton.

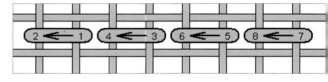

Backstitch.

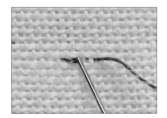

1. Make the first stitch, working right to left (1–2). Bring the needle back up at 3, two holes to the right of the first stitch, and form the second stitch by taking the needle down at 4, through the same hole as 1.

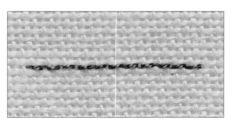

2. Continue working the rest of the row.

Running stitch

In this book, running stitch is used for basting the four sides of the design, and for stitching a vertical line down the centre of the fabric. Basting over and under two threads also helps with counting. Use a single strand of six-stranded cotton.

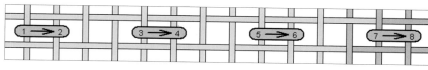

Running stitch.

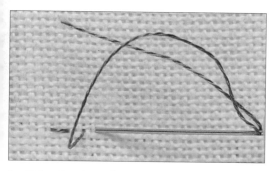

1. Take the thread over and under two fabric threads at a time to form a row of running stitch.

A row of running stitch.

Double running stitch

Double running stitch is also known as Holbein stitch, and was commonly featured on blackwork samplers. On the front of the work it looks the same as backstitch, but on the back it looks very different; double running stitch is identical on both sides of the fabric, and therefore gives a much neater finish on the back of your work than backstitch.

Begin by working running stitch from left to right, then complete the stitch by working in the opposite direction and filling in the gaps.

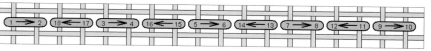

Double running stitch.

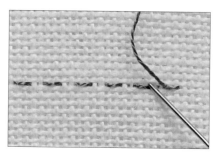

1. Work a row of running stitch, then begin to work back in the opposite direction, placing stitches in between those in the first row.

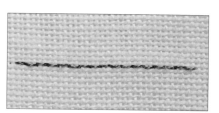

2. Continue working to the end of the row.

Cross stitch

Cross stitch is one of the oldest and most commonly used stitches. There are two possible sequences for stitching cross stitch. The first, which is recommended when using overdyed threads, is to complete each individual cross stitch before moving on to the next, working left to right. In the following demonstration I have used two strands of six-stranded variegated cotton.

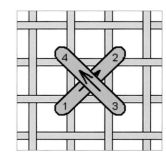

A single cross stitch.

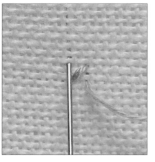
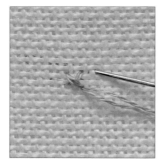
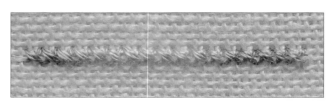

1. Work the first leg of the cross from bottom left to top right, then work the second leg over it from bottom right to top left.

2. To start the second stitch, bring the needle up at 3, through the same hole as the first stitch, and take the thread diagonally across to form the first leg of stitch two.

3. Continue the row, completing each cross stitch before moving on to the next. Notice the gradual change in colour as you progress along the row.

An alternative method of working cross stitch is to stitch a row of half crosses, and then to complete them when working back again in the opposite direction. This method is not suitable when working with overdyed threads.

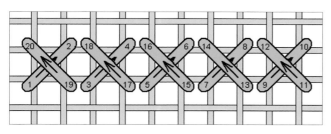
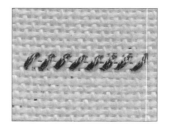

1. Working left to right, complete the first row of stitches. Work only one diagonal of each stitch, from bottom left to top right.

Cross stitch, working half cross stitches in one direction, and completing them in the opposite direction.

2. Work back along the row, from right to left, completing each cross stitch with the bottom right to top left diagonal.

Tip
For a more delicate look, cross stitch can also be worked over one thread.

Three-quarter cross stitch

There are four different ways of working this form of cross stitch, which can be used to add finer detail to a design.

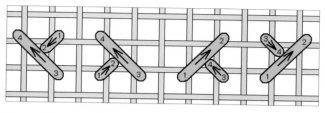

Four variations on three-quarter cross stitch.

Four completed three-quarter cross stitches, showing the different variations.

Smyrna cross

This stitch is also known as a double cross. It consists of a cross stitch with an upright cross stitch worked over the top, over either two threads or four. Being slightly raised, the stitch gives extra dimension and texture to your work. For added interest, it can be worked in two colours – one for the base cross and a second for the upright cross.

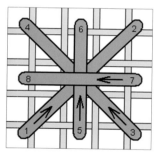

Large Smyrna cross, worked over four threads.

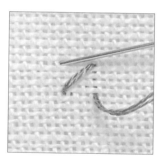

1. Work the first stitch diagonally over four threads (1–2), then work the second stitch (3–4).

2. Work the vertical leg of the upright cross from bottom to top.

3. Complete the Smyrna cross with the horizontal leg worked right to left.

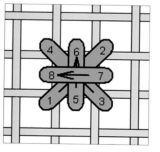

Small Smyrna cross, worked over two threads.

A completed Smyrna cross, worked over two threads.

33

Double herringbone stitch

This stitch consists of two rows of basic herringbone stitch interlaced together. It is very effective when worked in two colours – stitch the darker colour first, and then add the second row in the lighter colour.

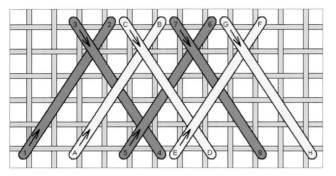

Double herringbone stitch.

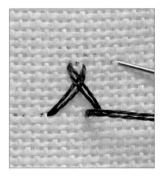

1. Work the first stitch from 1 to 2, taking the thread diagonally across four vertical and six horizontal fabric threads. Work the second stitch in the opposite direction, from 3 to 4, to create an inverted V shape.

2. Keeping an even tension, bring the working thread back through the fabric two holes to the left at 5, and take the needle down at 6 to form the next stitch.

3. Complete the first row of herringbone stitch.

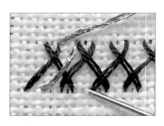

4. Change to a different coloured thread, and work the second row, placing the stitches in between those in the first row, and sharing the same fabric holes.

The completed double herringbone stitch.

Alternating Scotch stitch

This stitch, also known as diagonal satin stitch, flat stitch or cushion stitch, consists of solid blocks of embroidery. Each block comprises seven stitches worked over four fabric threads, all in the same diagonal direction. The second block in a row is a mirror image of the first and shares the same holes in the fabric; there are no gaps between the blocks. Rows are worked from left to right, alternating the blocks. For this demonstration, I have used two strands of six-stranded embroidery cotton.

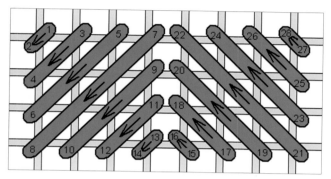

Alternating Scotch stitch.

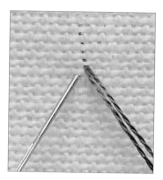

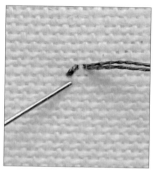

1. Bring the needle up through the fabric at 1, and take it back down the next hole along on the diagonal at 2.

2. Pull the thread through to make the first stitch. Make the second stitch in the same way, bringing the needle up through the fabric one hole along to the right at 3, and back down one hole lower at 4.

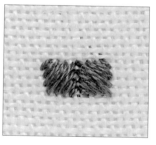

3. Make a further two stitches, moving one hole across and down each time.

4. Work the other side of the block with a further three stitches (9–14). Bring the thread up through the fabric two holes along to the right, ready to start of the second block of alternating Scotch stitch.

5. Work the second block as a mirror image of the first, taking the needle down through the same holes as the first block.

6. Continue along the row, alternating the blocks.

Four-sided stitch

This stitch is also known as square openwork. It can be worked with a normal tension or as a pulled thread stitch. When working this stitch as a pulled thread stitch, you will need to pull each leg as the needle comes up through the fabric to obtain a lacy effect; the tighter you pull the thread, the lacier the final effect will be. I have used a Perle cotton in this demonstration, as the thread needs to be pulled quite taut.

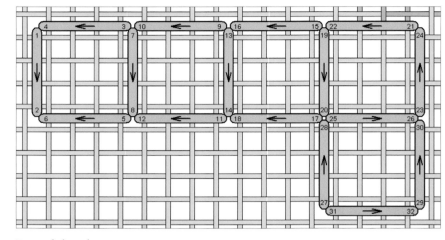

Four-sided stitch.

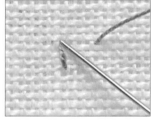

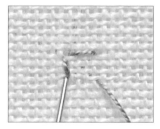

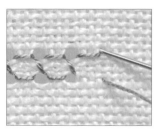

1. Work the first stitch (1–2) over four horizontal threads, pulling the stitch tight. Take the thread diagonally across the back of the fabric and bring it up at 3, then take the needle down at 4, through the same hole as 1.

2. Tighten the thread, take the thread diagonally across the back of the fabric and bring it up at 5, then take the needle down at 6, through the same hole as 2.

3. Pull the thread tight, and complete the fourth side of the square (7–8). This forms the first side of the next square. Continue working along the row.

4. To turn a corner, you need to work the side of the square that will be joined to the next square last. In this case, make the stitch at the top of the square, then work the right-hand vertical stitch from bottom to top.

5. Take the thread across to the bottom left-hand corner, and work the stitch at the bottom of the square from left to right.

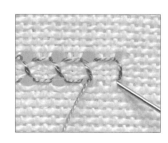

6. Form the next square below the last one following the order of the stitches shown in the diagram (27–32).

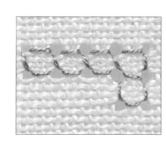

Three-sided stitch

This stitch is also known as Turkish lace. It is a triangular pulled stitch, worked from right to left. Each leg is worked twice, and the threads need to be pulled firmly to obtain the pattern. I have used a Perle cotton in this demonstration.

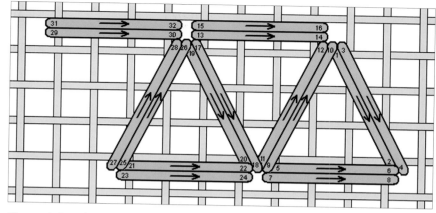

Three-sided stitch.

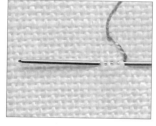

1. Begin with the right-hand side of the first triangle. Work two stitches from top to bottom (1–2 and 3–4), passing the second stitch through the same holes as the first. Tighten the thread, and bring the needle up four vertical threads to the left.

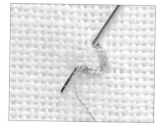

2. Work the two stitches at the base of the triangle, pulling the thread taut each time, and position the needle at the start of the next stitch.

3. Work this stitch twice, bringing the needle back through to the front of the fabric four vertical threads to the left, ready to start of the next triangle (13).

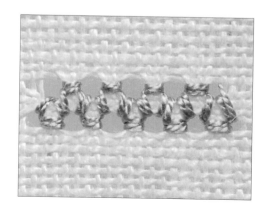

4. Continue along the row.

Satin stitch

Satin stitch is a block of straight stitches worked closely together to make a solid filling with a smooth texture. The length of each stitch, and the direction of the stitches, can vary, and the stitches can be worked horizontally, vertically or diagonally to create the desired shape. Try to keep the stitches smooth and do not let the threads twist; using a laying tool might help you keep an even tension (see page 11).

Below I have demonstrated a basic satin stitch, and provided diagrams for some variations. Start at the dot and work each stitch in the direction of the arrow.

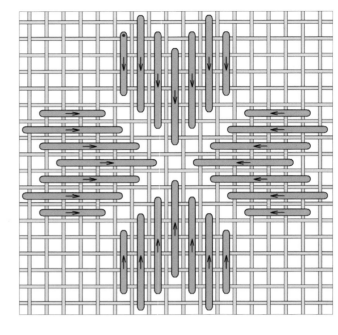

Large satin stitch flower. A smaller version can be made by reducing the number of threads over which you work each stitch.

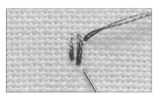

1. Sew each petal using straight stitches worked from top to bottom, following the diagram.

A completed petal.

Railroading

Passing the needle between two threads keeps the threads parallel.

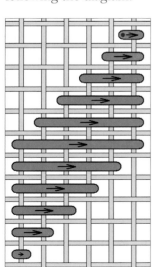
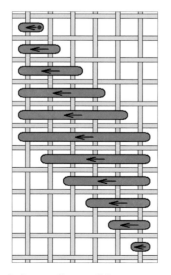

Satin stitch leaves. Both can be worked vertically as well by turning the diagram clockwise through 90°.

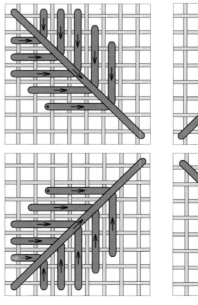

Modified satin stitch leaves. In each case, work the long diagonal stitch last.

Satin stitch blocks

These are used as security stitches worked over four fabric threads at either end of a block of drawn threads (see page 15). They wrap around the fabric threads so that they can be safely cut. The stitches are worked side by side, and all in the same direction, using either Perle cotton 5 with 25ct fabric, or Perle cotton 8 with 28ct fabric. You need to begin stitching with enough cotton to complete the whole block; never begin a new thread within a block of stitches.

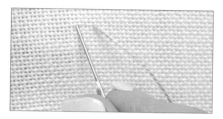

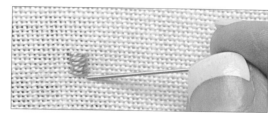

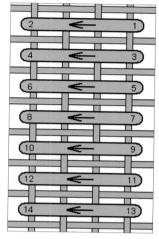

1. Bring the needle up through the fabric and pass the thread over four vertical fabric threads.

2. Pull the thread through and work the subsequent stitches in the same way, each time moving down by one fabric thread.

Satin stitch block.

Modified satin stitch blocks are also security stitches, consisting of four blocks of satin stitches that share fabric holes where they meet in the centre. **Right-angle satin stitch blocks** are two rows of security stitches going horizontally and vertically over the fabric to form a right-angled shape.

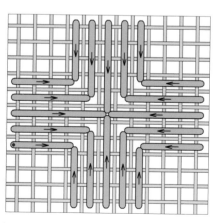

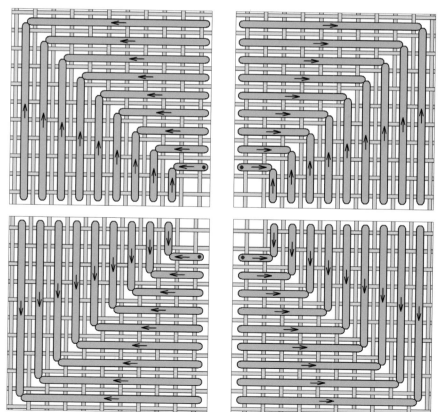

Modified satin stitch block. Start stitching at the dot and work each stitch in the direction of the arrow.

Right-angle satin stitch block. Start stitching at the dot and work each stitch in the direction of the arrow.

Summer Garden

Traditional whitework samplers from the seventeenth century featured drawn thread work. This embroidery features traditional techniques and stitches but is worked in contemporary colours using an overdyed thread together with Perle and stranded cotton. The beads add extra dimension and texture to the design.

The fabric threads are not cut and reweaved in this project; instead I have used satin stitch blocks as the security stitches, and the fabric threads are cut and removed.

This embroidery is stitched on Antique White Cashel 28ct linen by Zweigart, and measures 36 stitches horizontally and 142 stitches vertically. It has a finished size of 6.5 x 25.8cm (2.6 x 10.2in). Cut the linen to 23 x 41.5cm (9 x 16in) for framing. All stitches are worked with two strands of thread unless otherwise stated; backstitch is worked with one strand of thread. Each square on the chart represents two threads of fabric.

You will need

Antique White 28ct linen

DMC 712 Cream Perle cotton 8

DMC 712 Cream Perle cotton 12

■ DMC 523 Light Ash Green stranded cotton

■ DMC 524 Very Light Ash Green stranded cotton

■ DMC 778 Antique Mauve stranded cotton

□ Caron Waterlilies Rose Quartz overdyed thread

⊙ Mill Hill Cream seed beads 00123

To make your embroidery into a bell pull, cut a piece of card or buckram slightly larger than the finished design to allow for a border. Cover this with a piece of interlining or wadding, and then with a piece of lining fabric. Place this backing underneath the embroidery and pin it in place. Make sure you centre the design on the backing. Turn the bell pull over, and pin on the main backing fabric (this could be a piece of linen, silk or satin). Make sure the sides of the embroidery and the backing fabric are turned in neatly, particularly the corners. Stitch the backing fabric in place using a matching silk or cotton thread. For the decorative edging, sew a string of beads around the edge of the bell pull, adding a loop at the base and a fine chain at the top.

41

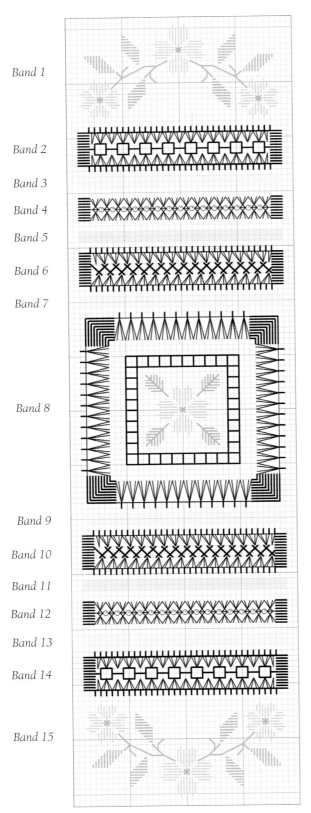

Band 1

Satin stitch the central flower and the two smaller outer flowers with two strands of DMC 778 (see page 38). Work a Smyrna cross (see page 33) in the centre of each flower with two strands of DMC 523. Backstitch the stems with one strand of DMC 523 (see page 30). Satin stitch the leaves with two strands of DMC 523 (see page 38).

Band 2

This part of the design is worked in diamond hemstitch (see page 23) over sixteen horizontal threads. For clarity, these horizontal threads are now numbered 1 to 16 from top to bottom.

1. Work two satin stitch blocks (see page 39) with one strand of DMC 712 Perle cotton 8. Each block consists of thirteen satin stitches covering twelve horizontal fabric threads, as indicated on the chart. Double check that between these two satin stitch blocks there are sixty-four vertical threads and twelve horizontal threads before you cut any fabric threads! Starting at the right-hand side, cut threads 3–6 (see page 15). Leave threads 7–10 uncut, then cut the next four horizontal threads 11–14. Turn the fabric 180° and cut the threads on the left-hand side to match. Carefully remove the loose fabric threads.

2. Work hemstitching over threads 15 and 16 (see page 18) with one strand of DMC 712 Perle cotton 12. Turn the fabric 180° and work a second row over threads 1 and 2.

3. Complete the centre four uncut threads (7–10) by stitching a diamond hemstitch (see page 23) with one strand of DMC 712 Perle cotton 12. Begin the diamond hemstitch at the right-hand side. Note that the first and last stitch in this band are modified and stitched over two threads not four. Work along the row to the left-hand side and finish the thread into the satin stitches. Turn the fabric 180° to work the second row. The stitches are a mirror image of the first row.

Band 3

Work alternating Scotch stitch (see page 35) with two strands of Caron Waterlilies Rose Quartz overdyed thread, as indicated on the chart.

Band 4

Work interlaced hemstitch with beads (see page 22) over eight horizontal threads. For clarity, these threads are now numbered 1 to 8 from top to bottom.

1. Work two satin stitch blocks (see page 39), each consisting of nine satin stitches covering eight fabric threads as indicated on the chart. Use one strand of DMC 712 Perle cotton 8. Double check that there are sixty-four vertical threads and eight horizontal threads between the two satin stitch blocks before you cut the fabric threads. Cut and remove the eight horizontal threads (see page 15).

2. Work interlaced hemstitch with beads (see page 22) with one strand of DMC 712 Perle cotton 12, placing a bead between each group of four threads.

Band 5

Work alternating Scotch stitch (see page 35) with two strands of DMC 524.

Band 6

Work herringbone stitch (see page 24) over sixteen horizontal threads. For clarity, these horizontal threads are now numbered 1 to 16 from top to bottom.

1. Work two satin stitch blocks (see page 39) with one strand of DMC 712 Perle cotton 8. Each block consists of thirteen satin stitches covering twelve horizontal fabric threads, as indicated on the chart. Double check that between these two satin stitch blocks there are sixty-four vertical threads and twelve horizontal threads before you cut any fabric threads. Cut threads 3–6 (see page 15) on the right-hand side first. Leave threads 7–10 uncut. Cut the next four horizontal threads, 11–14. Turn the fabric 180° and complete the left-hand side to match. Carefully remove the loose fabric threads.

2. Work hemstitching over threads 15 and 16 (see page 18) with one strand of DMC 712 Perle cotton 12. Turn the fabric 180° and work a second row over threads 1 and 2.

3. Complete the centre four uncut threads, 7–10, by stitching herringbone stitch (see page 24) with one strand of DMC 712 Perle cotton 8. Begin at the left-hand side and bring the needle up just below the fifth satin stitch to begin stitching. To finish the row, secure the thread in the satin stitch blocks on the reverse of the fabric.

Band 7

As for Band 3.

Band 8

The centre square is worked over seventy-two threads. In this section you will be cutting both horizontal and vertical threads, so you must take care with your counting before you begin to cut any fabric threads!

1. Work four sets of right-angle satin stitch blocks (see page 39) as indicated on the chart. Use one strand of DMC 712 Perle cotton 8. The first block is four threads down from Band 7, and two threads in from the margin. Check that there are forty-eight threads between the right-angle satin stitch blocks vertically and horizontally. Do not cut any fabric threads yet!

2. Work four-sided stitch (see page 36) with one strand of DMC 712 Perle cotton 12. Pull each stitch firmly as your needle comes up through the fabric to form the pattern.

3. Satin stitch the large flower (see page 38) with two strands of DMC 778. Work a Smyrna cross (see page 33) with two strands of DMC 523. Work the four modified satin stitch leaves (see page 38) with two strands of DMC 523.

4. Cut and remove the eight vertical threads between the top and bottom right-angle satin stitch blocks (see page 15). Cut and remove the eight horizontal threads between the right and left right-angle satin stitch blocks. The centre square is now formed.

5. Work hemstitch over four threads (see page 19) with one strand of DMC 712 Perle cotton 12 around the outer edge of the square. You will need to work each of the four sides individually. Do not take the thread over the satin stitch blocks.

Band 9

As for Band 3.

Band 10

As for Band 6.

Band 11

As for Band 5.

Band 12

As for Band 4.

Band 13

As for Band 3.

Band 14

As for Band 2.

Band 15

As for Band 1.

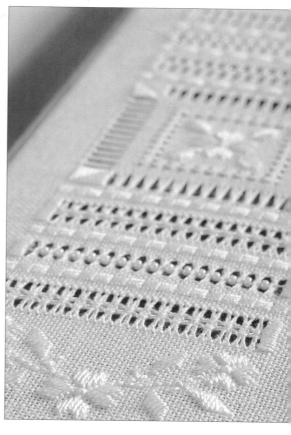

To stitch the traditional whitework version of this sampler, substitute the Antique White 28ct linen for White 28ct linen. Instead of DMC 712 Perle cotton 8, DMC 523 stranded cotton and DMC 778 stranded cotton, use DMC Blanc Perle cotton 8; and instead of DMC 712 Perle cotton 12, DMC 524 stranded cotton and Caron Waterlilies Rose Quartz overdyed thread, use DMC Blanc Perle cotton 12. Substitute the cream beads for white beads. When working with the Perle cotton, use only one strand of thread.

The embroidery is framed in a blue frame with a matching blue mount, which highlights the delicate, white stitching.

Roses and Lace

This project combines drawn thread techniques with counted thread embroidery stitches to create a stunning sampler. Beads and metallic threads enhance the embroidery by adding extra sparkle and dimension.

The sampler is stitched on White Cashel 28ct linen by Zweigart, and measures 66 stitches horizontally and 107 stitches vertically. The finished size is 12 x 19.4cm (4.7 x 7.6in). For framing, cut the linen to 28 x 35.5cm (11 x 14in).

Cross stitch with two strands of thread unless otherwise specified, and backstitch with one strand of thread. Each square on the chart represents two threads of fabric.

You will need

White 28ct linen
- Kreinik 001 Silver Very Fine Braid No. 4
- DMC 208 Very Dark Lavender stranded cotton
- DMC 210 Medium Lavender stranded cotton
- DMC 211 Light Lavender stranded cotton
- DMC 501 Dark Green stranded cotton

  DMC Blanc stranded cotton for sewing on the beads

  DMC Blanc Perle cotton 12

  DMC Blanc Perle cotton 8
- Mill Hill Silver seed beads 02010
- Mill Hill Dark Mauve seed beads 62042
- Mill Hill Light Mauve seed beads 62047

I have mounted this embroidery on a purple mountboard, which coordinates with the embroidery and highlights the white drawn thread work. The silver frame reflects the silver thread which, together with the beads, add depth and sparkle to the design.

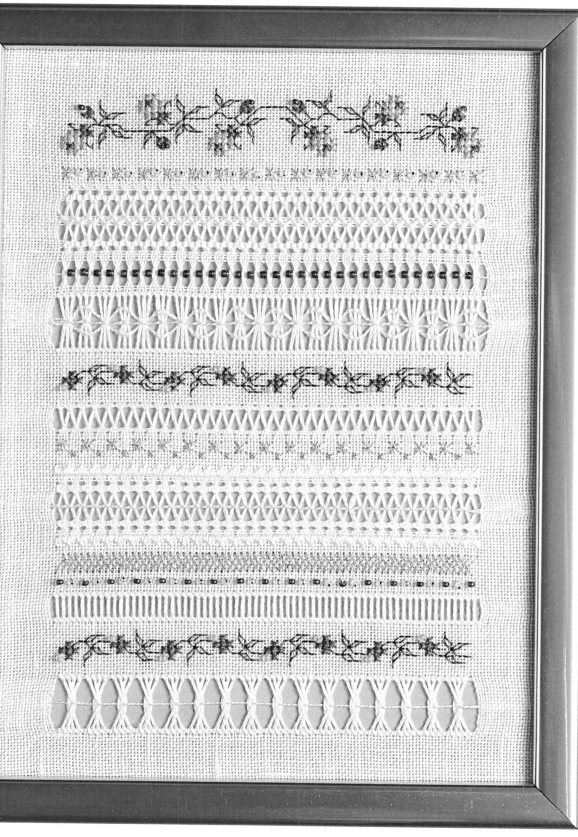

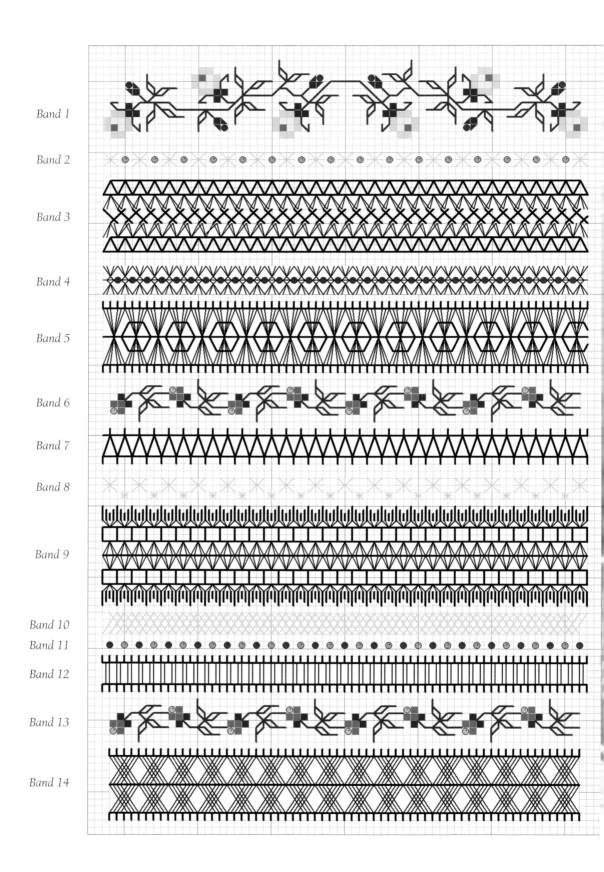

Band 1

Band 2

Band 3

Band 4

Band 5

Band 6

Band 7

Band 8

Band 9

Band 10

Band 11

Band 12

Band 13

Band 14

Band 1

Backstitch (see page 30) the stems and leaves with one strand of DMC 501. Work the flowers using DMC 208, 210, 211 and 501 in cross stitch (see page 32) and three-quarter cross stitch (see page 33), signified by solid squares and half-solid squares respectively. Add the Dark Mauve beads (see page 29) as indicated on the chart.

Band 2

Work Smyrna crosses over four threads (see page 33) with one strand of Silver Very Fine Braid No.4. Add the Silver beads as indicated on the chart.

Band 3

Work this band in three-sided (see page 37) and herringbone stitch (see page 24) over twenty horizontal threads. For clarity, these horizontal threads are now numbered 1 to 20 from top to bottom.

1. Begin this row at the right-hand side of the sampler. With one strand of DMC Blanc Perle cotton 12, work three-sided stitch (see page 37) over threads 1–4. Work each leg twice and pull the stitches firmly to obtain the pattern.

2. Work a second row of three-sided stitch over threads 17–20. These two rows must be stitched before any of the threads are cut.

3. You are now ready to cut and remove threads 5 and 7 (see page 14), and reweave threads 6 and 8. Threads 9–12 remain uncut. Cut and remove threads 13 and 15 and reweave threads 14 and 16 as before.

4. Work herringbone stitch (see page 24) over horizontal threads 9–12, with one strand of DMC Blanc Perle cotton 8. Begin the row at the left-hand side, by bringing the needle and thread up between horizontal threads 8 and 9.

Band 4

Work this band in interlaced hemstitch with beads (see page 22) over eight horizontal threads. For clarity, these horizontal threads are now numbered 1 to 8 from top to bottom.

1. Cut and remove threads 1, 3, 5 and 7 and reweave threads 2, 4, 6 and 8 (see page 14).

2. Work interlaced hemstitch with beads (see page 22) with one strand of DMC Blanc Perle cotton 12. Place a Dark Mauve bead between each group of threads. These beads must be added as the row is worked.

Band 5

This band consists of modified coral knot clusters (see page 26) worked over twenty horizontal threads. For clarity, these horizontal threads are now numbered 1 to 20 from top to bottom.

1. Cut and remove threads 3, 5, 7, 9, 11, 13, 15 and 17 and reweave threads 4, 6, 8, 10, 12, 14, 16 and 18 (see page 14).

2. Work hemstitch over threads 19 and 20 (see page 18) with one strand of DMC Blanc Perle cotton 12. Turn the fabric 180° and complete a second row of hemstitch over threads 1 and 2.

3. Work modified coral knot clusters (see page 26) with one strand of DMC Blanc Perle cotton 8.

Band 6

Take care, as this band begins and ends two threads in from the margin. Backstitch (see page 30) the stems and leaves with one strand of DMC 501. Work the flowers using DMC 208 in cross stitch (see page 32), and add the Light Mauve beads (see page 29) as indicated on the chart.

Band 7

Work zig zag hemstitch (see page 20) over ten horizontal threads. For clarity, these horizontal threads are now numbered 1 to 10.

1. Cut and remove threads 3, 5 and 7 and reweave threads 4, 6 and 8 (see page 14).

2. Work zig zag hemstitch (see page 20) with one strand of DMC Blanc Perle cotton 12.

Band 8

Work Smyrna crosses over four threads and over two threads (see page 33) with one strand of Silver Very Fine Braid No. 4.

Band 9

Work four-sided stitch (see page 36) and coral knots (see page 25) over twenty-eight horizontal threads. For clarity, these horizontal threads are now numbered 1 to 28 from top to bottom.

1. Work satin stitch over threads 1, 2, 3 and 4 and threads 25, 26, 27 and 28 as indicated on the chart. Use one strand of DMC Blanc Perle cotton 8.

2. Work four-sided stitch (see page 36) over threads 7, 8, 9 and 10. Work a second row of four-sided stitch over threads 19, 20, 21 and 22. Work both these rows of four-sided stitch with one strand of DMC Blanc Perle cotton 12. These rows must be completed before any threads are cut and rewoven.

3. Cut and remove threads 11, 13, 15 and 17 and reweave threads 12, 14, 16 and 18 (see page 14).

4. Work coral knots (see page 25) with one strand of DMC Blanc Perle cotton 8.

Band 10

Work double herringbone stitch (see page 34) using Kreinik Silver Very Fine Braid No. 4 for the first row and one strand of DMC 210 for the second row.

Band 11

Add the row of alternating Dark Mauve and Silver beads (see page 29) as indicated on the chart.

Band 12

This band is worked in ladder stitch (see page 19) over ten horizontal threads. For clarity, these horizontal threads are now numbered 1 to 10 from top to bottom.

1. Cut and remove threads 3, 5 and 7 and reweave threads 4, 6 and 8 (see page 14).

2. Work ladder stitch (see page 19) over threads 1 and 2 and threads 9 and 10 with one strand of DMC Blanc Perle cotton 12.

Band 13

As for Band 6.

Band 14

Take care, as this band begins and ends two threads in from the margin. Work interlaced hemstitch over twenty horizontal threads. For clarity, these horizontal threads are now numbered 1 to 20 from top to bottom.

1. Cut and remove threads 3, 5, 7, 9, 11, 13, 15 and 17 and reweave threads 4, 6, 8, 10, 12, 14, 16 and 18 (see page 14).

2. Work hemstitching (see page 18) over threads 19 and 20 with one strand of DMC Blanc Perle cotton 12. Turn the fabric 180° and complete a second row of hemstitching over threads 1 and 2.

3. Work interlaced hemstitch (see page 21) with one strand of DMC Blanc Perle cotton 8.

To stitch this sampler in the second colourway shown opposite, substitute the White 28ct linen for Confederate Grey 28ct linen. In Band 4 step 2, Band 5 step 2 and Band 7 step 2, use DMC 928 Perle cotton 12 instead of the suggested thread, and use DMC 928 stranded cotton for sewing on the beads.

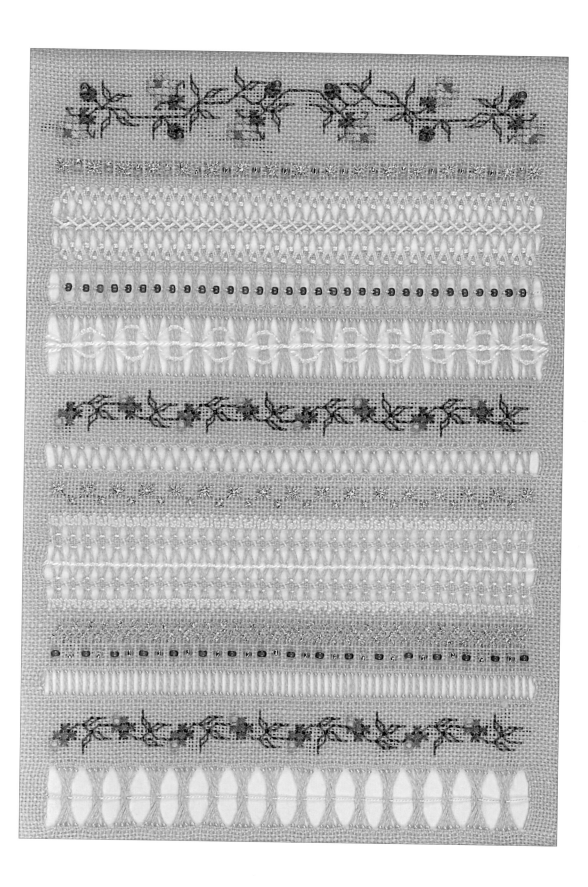

Flower Garland

This design is worked in silk threads, which are gorgeous to work with. It can be framed, stitched into a decorative cushion, or used to decorate a box top. For this project, I have used the blue and green colourway as a box top and the pink and green variation (see pages 56–57) has been stitched into a cushion.

The embroidery is stitched on Antique White 25ct Dublin Linen by Zweigart and measures 88 stitches horizontally by 88 stitches vertically. The finished size is 17.9 x 17.9cm (7 x 7in), and the linen should be cut to 33 x 33cm (13 x 13in) for framing.

All the stitches are worked with one strand of thread. Work the cross-stitched borders after the cutting and reweaving of the fabric threads has been completed, add the treasures once the sampler is finished. Each square on the chart represents two threads of fabric.

You will need

Antique White 25ct linen
- Kreinik 002 Gold Fine Braid No. 8

  DMC 712 Cream Perle cotton 5

  DMC 712 Cream Perle cotton 8

  DMC 712 Cream Perle cotton 12

  DMC 712 stranded cotton for attaching the treasures
- Kreinik 5204 Blue Silk Serica
- Kreinik 4166 Green Silk Serica
- Two packets of Blue Mill Hill Crystal Treasures 13033

Purpose-made boxes with an aperture lid in which to mount your embroidery are widely available in a range of shapes and sizes. The one I have used for this project measures 22.5cm (9in) square, with an 18cm (7in) square aperture. It comes with a piece of card on which to mount your embroidery, and I usually add a layer of wadding or interlining, and then a piece of lining fabric on top of the card to give the embroidery a soft and slightly raised finish. The instructions are the same as those provided for the bell pull on page 41.

53

The centre square

Begin stitching at the centre of the design. Work the four sets of modified satin stitch blocks (see page 39) with one strand of DMC 712 Cream Perle cotton 5. Before you start to cut the fabric threads, double check that there are sixteen threads between the modified satin stitch blocks both vertically and horizontally. Cut and remove the four vertical threads between the top and bottom modified satin stitch blocks (see page 15). Cut and remove the four horizontal threads between the right and left modified satin stitch blocks. Work ladder stitch (see page 19) with one strand of DMC 712 Perle cotton 12. The centre square is now completed.

The flower garland

Work the satin stitch leaves (see page 38) and backstitch the stems (see page 30) with one strand of Kreinik 4166 Green Silk Serica. Work the satin stitch flowers, including the centre flower (see page 38), with one strand of Kreinik 5204 Blue Silk Serica.

Four-sided stitch border

Work the four-sided stitch border (see page 36) with one strand of DMC 712 Perle cotton 12.

Outer drawn thread area

1. This area is over twenty threads. With careful counting, begin to cut and reweave the threads (see

page 14). As this is a square design, you will be cutting both horizontal and vertical threads. Once the preparation work is finished, you will have four square holes in between the fabric threads.

2. Work hemstitching (see page 18) with one strand of DMC 712 Perle cotton 12. Work both the outside and inside edge. Work each side individually and do not take the thread across the corners.

3. Work the interlaced hemstitch (see page 21) with one strand of DMC 712 Perle cotton 8. Secure the working threads in the margin. These threads will form a cross in the square holes and become part of the woven corner.

4. Work the woven wheels in each of the four corners (see page 28) with one strand of DMC 712 Perle cotton 8.

Gold borders

Finally, work the gold borders in cross stitch (see page 32) with one strand of Gold Fine Braid No. 8, as indicated on the chart.

To finish

Add the crystal treasures as indicated on the chart with one strand of DMC 712 stranded cotton.

To stitch the design for the cushion, use Kreinik 032 Pearl Fine Braid No. 8 instead of Gold; DMC Blanc Perle cotton 8 instead of DMC 712 Perle cotton 8 and DMC Blanc Perle cotton 12 instead of DMC 712 Perle cotton 12; Kreinik 3044 Pink Silk Serica instead of 5204 Blue and Kreinik 4163 Green Silk Serica instead of 4166 Green; and Kreinik 8000 White Silk Serica instead of DMC 712 Perle cotton 5. Substitute Mill Hill Crystal Treasures 13033 for Mill Hill Crystal Treasures 13021, and replace the centre flower and crystal treasure with a Mill Hill Glass Treasure 12182. To sew on the treasures, use DMC Blanc stranded cotton instead of DMC 712 stranded cotton.

To make the cushion, you need an inner pad measuring 20.5cm (8in) square and two pieces of satin or silk each measuring 23.5cm (9in) square. This allows 1.5cm (½in) all round for seams. Cut around the embroidery to within 2cm (1in) of the stitching, and gently press the seams under to form a neat square. Pin the embroidery on to one of the pieces of satin or silk, making sure it is centred all the way round. Stitch it in place using a small blind stitch. With the wrong sides together, pin and sew around the outside of the cushion, 1.5cm (½in) in from the edge. Leave a gap in the bottom large enough to push the pad through. Turn the cushion in the right way and insert the pad. Pin and hand stitch the gap at the bottom. Sew a row of beading around the outside of the cushion to cover the seams.

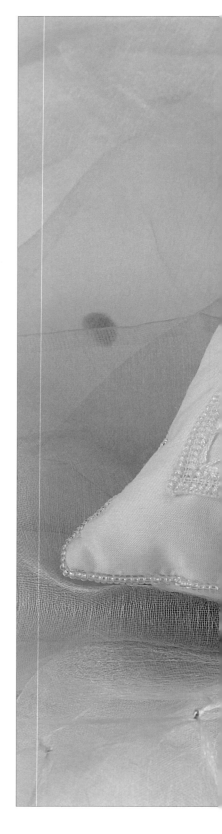

Rosebud Trellis

This project can be stitched in two colourways using gorgeous metallic threads and beads mixed with traditional Perle and stranded cotton threads. The design features drawn thread work with counted thread embroidery stitches to create this unique sampler.

The fabric threads are not cut and reweaved in this project; instead satin stitch blocks are used as the security stitches, and the fabric threads cut and removed.

The embroidery is stitched on Cream Cashel 28ct linen by Zweigart, and measures 98 stitches horizontally and 129 stitches vertically. The finished size is 17.8 x 22.9cm (7 x 9in). Cut the linen to 33 x 38cm (13 x 15in) for framing.

Cross stitch is worked with two strands of thread unless otherwise stated; backstitch is worked with one strand of thread. Each square on the chart represents two threads of fabric.

You will need

Cream 28ct linen
- Kreinik 002 Gold Fine Braid No. 8
- DMC 223 Medium Shell Pink stranded cotton
- DMC 520 Ash Green stranded cotton
  DMC 712 Cream Perle cotton 8
  DMC 712 Cream Perle cotton 12
- Mill Hill Gold petite beads 40557
- Mill Hill Cream seed beads 00123
  DMC 712 stranded cotton for sewing on the beads

Colour is an important aspect of any design. The richness of this embroidery is enhanced by the use of both gold threads and gold beads, and the green frame reflects the green leaves and stems of the rosebud trellis.

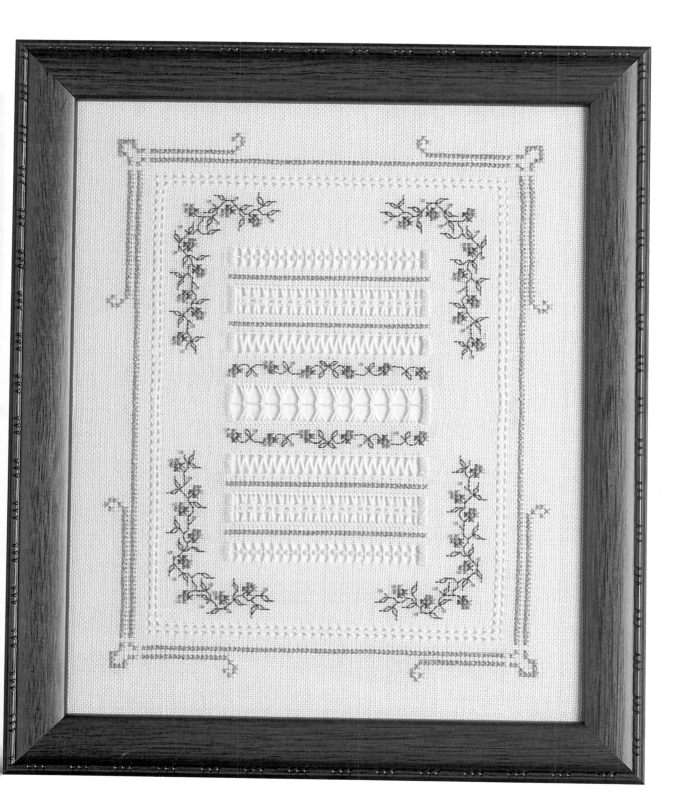

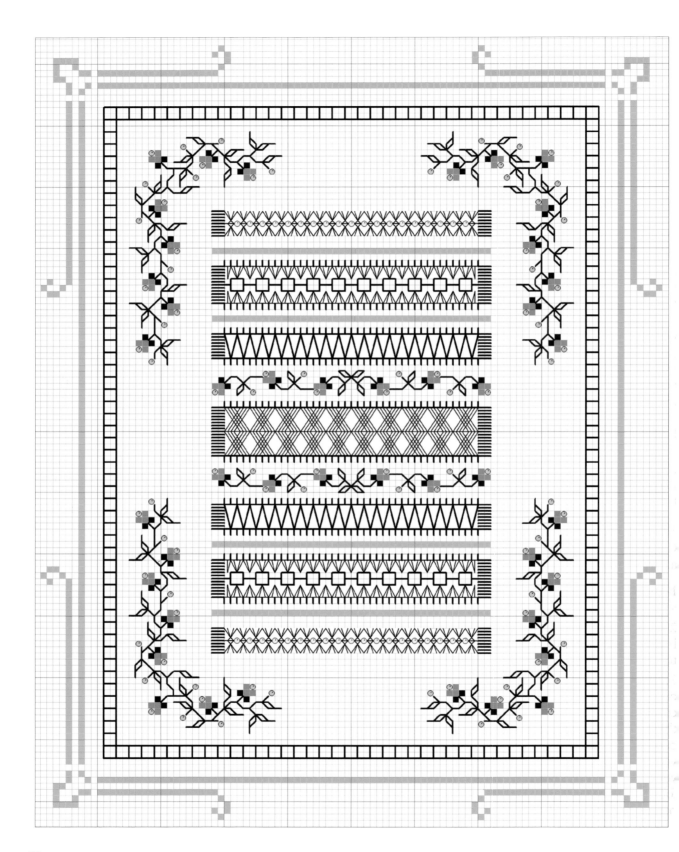

Border

1. Cross stitch the gold border (see page 32) as indicated on the chart using Gold Fine Braid No. 8.

2. Work the four-sided stitch border (see page 36) with one strand of DMC 712 Perle cotton 12.

3. Backstitch (see page 30) the stems and leaves with one strand of DMC 520 stranded cotton. Work the flowers using DMC 223 and 520 in cross stitch.

4. Attach the Gold petite beads 40557 (see page 29) as indicated on the chart.

Band 1

Work interlaced hemstitch with beads (see page 22) over eight horizontal threads. For clarity, these horizontal threads are now numbered 1 to 8 from top to bottom.

1. Work two blocks of satin stitches (see page 39) with one strand of DMC 712 Perle cotton 8. These each consist of nine satin stitches covering eight fabric threads, as indicated on the chart. Double check that there are eighty vertical threads and eight horizontal threads between the two satin stitch blocks before you cut the fabric threads. Cut and remove the eight horizontal threads (see page 15).

2. Work interlaced hemstitch with beads (see page 22) with one strand of DMC 712 Perle cotton 12, placing a Cream seed bead between each group of four threads.

Band 2

Cross stitch (see page 32) using Gold Fine Braid No. 8 as indicated on the chart.

Band 3

This band is stitched in diamond hemstitch (see page 23) over sixteen horizontal threads. For clarity, these horizontal threads are now numbered 1 to 16 from top to bottom.

1. Work two satin stitch blocks (see page 39) with one strand of DMC 712 Perle cotton 8. These each consist of thirteen satin stitches covering twelve fabric threads, as indicated on chart. Double check that between these two satin stitch blocks there are eighty vertical threads and twelve horizontal threads before you cut any fabric threads (see page 15). Cut the first four horizontal threads (threads 3–6) on the right-hand side first. Leave threads 7, 8, 9 and 10 uncut.

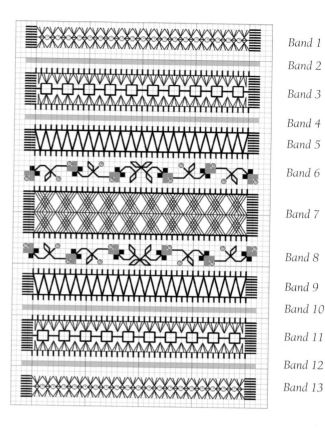

Band 1
Band 2
Band 3
Band 4
Band 5
Band 6
Band 7
Band 8
Band 9
Band 10
Band 11
Band 12
Band 13

Cut the next four horizontal threads (threads 11–14). Turn the fabric 180° to complete the left-hand side to match. Carefully remove the loose fabric threads.

2. Work hemstitching over threads 15 and 16 (see page 18) with one strand of DMC 712 Perle cotton 12. Turn the fabric 180° and work a second row over threads 1 and 2.

3. The centre four uncut threads (7–10) are completed by stitching diamond hemstitch (see page 23) with one strand of DMC 712 Perle cotton 12. Begin the diamond hemstitch at the right-hand side. Note that the first and last stitches in this band are modified and stitched over two threads not four, as shown in the stitch diagram. Work along the row to the left-hand side and finish the thread into the satin stitches.

4. Turn the fabric 180° to work the second row. The stitches are a mirror image of the first row.

Band 4

As for Band 2.

Band 5

This band is zig zag hemstitch (see page 20) worked over twelve horizontal threads. For clarity, these horizontal threads are now numbered 1 to 12, from top to bottom.

1. Work two blocks of satin stitches (see page 39) with one strand of DMC 712 Perle cotton 8. These each consist of nine satin stitches covering eight fabric threads, as indicated on chart. Double check that there are eighty vertical threads and eight horizontal threads between the two satin stitch blocks before you cut the fabric threads. Cut and remove the eight horizontal threads (see page 15).

2. Work zig zag hemstitch (see page 20) over threads 11 and 12 with one strand of DMC 712 Perle cotton 12. Turn the fabric 180° and work the second row over threads 1 and 2.

Band 6

Cross stitch the flowers (see page 32) as indicated on the chart using DMC 223 and 520. Backstitch the stems and leaves (see page 30) with one strand of DMC 520 stranded cotton. Attach Gold petite beads (see page 29) as indicated on the chart.

Band 7

This band is worked in interlaced hemstitch (see page 21) over twenty horizontal threads. For clarity, these horizontal threads are now numbered 1 to 20, from top to bottom.

1. Work two satin stitch blocks (see page 39) with one strand of DMC 712 Perle cotton 8. These each consist of seventeen satin stitches covering sixteen fabric threads, as indicated on chart. Double check that between these two satin stitch blocks there are eighty vertical threads and sixteen horizontal threads before you cut the fabric. Cut and carefully remove the threads (see page 15).

2. Work hemstitch over threads 19 and 20 (see page 18) with one strand of DMC 712 Perle cotton 12. Turn the fabric 180° and work a second row over threads 1 and 2.

3. Work interlaced hemstitch (see page 21) with one strand of DMC 712 Perle cotton 8.

Band 8

As for Band 6.

Band 9

As for Band 5.

Band 10

As for Band 2.

Band 11

As for Band 3.

Band 12

As for Band 2.

Band 13

As for Band 1.

To stitch this design in the second colourway, use Kreinik 007 Pink Fine Braid No. 8 instead of Gold; use DMC 315 Antique Mauve stranded cotton instead of DMC 223 Medium Shell Pink and DMC 501 Dark Green stranded cotton instead of DMC 520 Ash Green; and substitute DMC 712 Perle cotton 8 for DMC 778 Perle cotton 8 and DMC 712 Perle cotton 12 for DMC 778 Perle cotton 12. Replace the Mill Hill Gold petite beads 40557 with Mill Hill Pink petite beads 40553, and the Mill Hill Cream seed beads 00123 Cream with Mill Hill Pale Pink seed beads 03051. For sewing on the beads use DMC 778 stranded cotton. The fabric used is Lavender Mist Cashel 28ct linen.

Index

7334